Out Of Africa
I Thought Christianity Was A White Man's Religion Until I Met Christ

Derek Grier

Ham Publishing Company
"And God blessed Noah and his sons, . . ."
Genesis 9:1

Unless otherwise indicated all scripture quotations are taken from the *New International Version* of the Bible.

All rights reserved under international copyright law. Written permission must be secured from the publisher to use or reproduce any part of this book.

FIRST EDITION

Ham Publishing Company
"And God blessed Noah and his sons,..."
Genesis 9:1

OUT OF AFRICA:
I Thought Christianity Was a White Man's Religion Until I Met Christ

ISBN 0-963-2169-2-9
Copyright ©1996 by Derek Grier
P.O. Box 73308 Washington, D.C. 20056-3308

Published by Ham Publishing Company
P.O. Box 73308
Washington, D.C. 20056-3308

Printed in the United States of America.

TABLE OF CONTENTS

Introduction 5

I. God My Redeemer. 7
Christianity a white man's religion? - Islam and the Nation of Islam - A vision of Jesus

II. God Who Ordains 27
Two unforgettable encounters - In the valley of decision

III. God My Sanctifier 45
Sedition - The pleasures of sin - The final surrender

IV. God My Vindicator. .55
Brother against brother - Fire from heaven - Learning to forgive

V. God My Banner. 71
The politics of preaching - An individual against an institution

VI. God Whom I Worship. 85
Final approach - Sweet success

INTRODUCTION

While still a campus minister at Howard University and while much of this story was unfolding, the Lord spoke to my heart. He said, "Bless my people with your life." He then cautioned me to tell even the parts I might feel guarded about.

Years have passed between this commission and its completion. Yet, as I walk the streets of our inner cities and look into the eyes of suffering people, I feel more than a sense of sorrow. I feel a burning responsibility. The least I can do is share with younger brothers what it cost me to become a man. My lesson is simple. Manhood is remaining true to one's righteous convictions and to the one true God in the face of challenge.

Out of Africa is not an attempt to write an extensive autobiography, as much as to use my personal experiences to bear witness to the fact that Jesus Christ transcends all our notions about race or any other supposed limitation. I was of the opinion that Christianity was a white man's religion until I actually met Christ. In spite of all the lies I had heard about Him, I discovered that Jesus loved me and that I did not need to dress in white face to be accepted by Him. The one who held the earth in the palm of His hand, yet emptied Himself of divine privilege to the point of being

Out of Africa

born in a reeking barn, understands what it is to be an underdog.

Because of my experience and the prevailing racial attitudes of our times, *Out of Africa* begins by discussing color but moves on quickly to discuss a more dominant issue, the development of character. Although, our contexts may differ, this story has a universal theme. A boy is baptized into the fires of life and becomes a man.

Dr. Martin Luther King once said, "The ultimate measure of a man is not where he stands in moments of comfort and convenience, but where he stands at times of challenge and controversy." This book is about the grace that God gives the human spirit to withstand and overcome. Apostle Paul wrote, **"Therefore put on the full armor of God, so that when the evil day comes, you may be able to stand your ground, and after you have done everything, to stand. Stand firm then . . ." (Ephesians 6:13-14)**

Reverend Derek Grier

ONE

GOD MY REDEEMER

Discussions about race cause some of the most impassioned reactions in America, today. On one side of town, the man of God stands with his finger pointing toward heaven and as the palm of his hand strikes the pulpit, he denounces minority concerns and calls them the "bloodsuckers" of the American dream. On the other side of town, the man of God stands behind his holy desk and with quivering intonations, he denounces racial injustice and all who would turn a blind eye to the suffering of the swarthy masses.

These realities are painful but so very common. At times, I would like to pretend that they do not exist but as an African American, this is impossible. As common as rock-n-roll and apple pie are to the white American experience, racism is to the African American experience. Hence, conversion for a black person who views Christianity as the faith of our nation can be problematic. As I take this journey and relive many of the emotions that I felt when I gave my life to the humble carpenter of Galilee, it is impossible for me not to start by sharing the history that made this almost impossible.

WHITE JESUS

My religious background was minimal. As a child, I occasionally attended Sunday school. I seldom enjoyed it because my teachers were unable and sometimes unwilling to answer my questions. Consequently, I viewed Christ as the God who slept through slavery. He was the spiritual benefactor of a nation that I felt hated people of my hue. His commonly depicted blue eyes, pasty face, stringy blond hair and sickly looking frame was pathetic. The Jesus portrayed on television could not have hung out with me for one night without getting beat up.

God My Redeemer

The closest I had come to faith in Christ was when I was in elementary school. My parents sent me to a christian summer camp and during the tabernacle service, we sang a song with lyrics something like this,

> "Jesus, Jesus, there's just something about that name. Master, Savior, Jesus. Let all heaven and earth proclaim. Kings and Kingdoms will all pass away but there is just something about that name."

As we sang, something seemed to cover me like an invisible, warm blanket. As quickly as it had come, it was gone. I did not know how to keep the blanket on. I think that if I had responded to this experience by praying a prayer of dedication, Jesus would have changed my life.

Albeit, another year, my parents sent both my brother and I to this predominantly white, Southern Baptist camp. This time, things were a little different. When my brother began to tan, the other white kids forcibly put toothpaste all over his face to make him fit in. This was not my first experience with racism. There were kids back in my own neighborhood whom I could not play with because I was black. Racism is sufferable but when put into a religious context, the sting is far more bitter.

Most people, white and black alike, at some point in their lives, come to the realization that the world is often a heartless place. The extent of man's inhumanity to man is sometimes shocking but we learn to live with this fact. Nonetheless, what has been crushing to the consciousness of African Americans is not our rejection by other races of people but the thought that we are lesser by eternal design. If somewhere in the recesses of the soul lives the idea that God, whose divine order cannot be amended, created people of color inferior to other peoples, ambition would seem futile and we would be doomed to moral poverty.

The horror of racism is not only found in the institution itself, as much as in its pseudo-christian footings. Millions upon millions of people have been systematically taught, by those considered to be the guardians of the Christian faith that God created people of African descent inferior to other races. Most Christians would disavow Hinduism outright but under the surface believe this idea of a genetic caste system. Nothing is as sinister as teaching a child that the God who made the oceans and the winds created them to be the subjects of a superior class of children.

God My Redeemer

Many in the white community wonder why groups that invert this doctrine and espouse that blacks are little gods and whites are little devils have such success. There is little else as seductive to the oppressed than to reclaim our sense of worth, even if it costs us a little common sense. In a large part, the Church instigates this behavior when we begin to extol America as a traditionally Christian nation. If our nation was ever Christian, we could only say so apologetically. Native Americans, African Americans, Jews, Asian Americans and other nonwhites suffered greatly in this so-called Christian nation. I tremble as I consider the fact that we must all stand before a holy God and answer for our shameless presumption.

By the time I became a teenager, being a Christian meant that I would have to wear toothpaste on my face to be accepted by a white man's God. For me, death would have been sweeter. My people were despised by Christians, so I rejected their Christ.

In spite of my attitude, God loved me. He would not permit me to be another victim of the "great deception." In America, perception is often elevated above fact and attitudes about race often defy reason. Nonetheless, God intended to redeem me from this vicious cycle of hate.

Behind the events of this chapter is the redemptive work of my Savior. Behind my arguments, He saw my need. As black as I was, as black as I am, He loved black me. What a revelation!

THIS IS IT

In 1983, I entered Howard University, in Washington, D.C. It was considered one of the best African American universities in the country. I was hungry to experience the best of my heritage. Furthermore, the lure of the University being in the nation's capital helped synch it.

As a freshman at Howard, I was introduced to a broad spectrum of new philosophies. For reasons already mentioned, Christianity was not attractive to me. Although, Dr. Martin Luther King and many others were considered Christian, I felt that they succeeded not because of their faith but in spite of it.

By my sophomore year in college, I began to read the Koran. I had heard that it was the African American alternative to the Bible. Although it had a dark quality to it, I began to study it because one of the champions of the

God My Redeemer

cause, Malcolm X, and my then fascination, Louis Farrakhan, taught about it. These men seemed to tell it like it was and did not flinch at the white establishment. I felt that integration was like crashing a party that I was not invited to and never would be. These men taught that we should be independent and proud. This struck a chord in me.

During the fall of my second year at Howard, while sitting in class, I began to feel burdened by something beyond my experience. It was overwhelming! I left my class early and went home and lay on my dormitory bed, trying to collect myself. The stirring inside me was beyond description.

What I felt was so big that I knew it had to be an experience with God. Somehow, I understood that the feeling embodied God's longing for my people. My eyes filled with tears as I writhed in discomfort. I suppose it could be likened to the feeling a mother would have who could not touch or hold her child or perhaps, the feeling a father would have while watching his child being harmed through a Plexiglas window, too thick to cross.

Suddenly, as if a person was standing just three feet away, I heard a voice say, "This is it!"

Out of Africa

Immediately, the pain left. I looked up to see who was speaking to me. I saw a man standing in a long, white, flowing robe. He stood in front of me just long enough for my faculties to overthrow my doubts of the reality of what was happening. Intuitively, I knew that this man was Jesus. Conceivably, it was because it was the same presence I sensed as a child, while singing the camp song.

I did not understand what His statement meant. However, it became clear that Jesus was the one I was looking for. I jumped off the floor and ran into the bathroom to wash the tears from my face. Then, my confidence lapsed and I searched the closets, the bathroom and even looked outside the front door, to make sure my roommates were not playing tricks on me.

About a year after this experience, in my junior year of college, I answered an altar call at the University's chapel and gave my life to Christ. At twenty years of age, I began the most challenging journey a person could dare undertake. I began to serve the God of Abraham, Isaac and Jacob. I became a disciple of the most controversial person in history - Jesus Christ.

With my background, the strategy of the

underworld to bewitch my yet, tender faith should be obvious. I could only follow the Christ after I resolved my leanings toward Islam. To avow Jesus means to disavow all else.

NATION OF ISLAM

A few months after my conversion, on the first national celebration of Dr. Martin Luther King's birthday, a radio broadcaster made a crude comment about the national holiday. When I arrived at the civil rights organization, where I worked, an associate told me the news.

When I heard what the Caucasian disc jockey had said, I was enraged. I was a very new Christian and understood very little about being led by the Holy Spirit and the scriptural definition of love. After a few minutes of pacing the floor, I got into my car and drove to the University.

I rounded up a few student leaders, went into the lower level of the student center and gave a speech. I prompted the students to organize. In about ten minutes, we had over a dozen students willing to picket the radio station.

A member of the Nation of Islam (NOI) and I became the head organizers. We demanded the firing of the disc jockey and picketed for several

Out of Africa

days. By the end of our demonstrations, we had organized close to two hundred students to carry picket signs. Unfortunately, some of the slogans against the disc jockey were as ugly as the comments that started the protest.

It was not long before the disc jockey apologized for making his slur. After an intense debate among the students, we decided not to settle for anything less than his job termination. This is where we went wrong. The spirit of protest should always be reconciliation.

The owner of the radio station had offered us the care of scholarship money, to show their good will toward the black community. We declined and I felt insulted. We considered it a bribe.

As the protest grew, the differences between my NOI counterparts and I began to surface. I became very disturbed by some of their Jew-bashing comments and attempts to grandstand versus any real plan to benefit our community. As things began to move in a direction that I was extremely uncomfortable with, I began to give over the leadership of the protest to the NOI student leader.

God My Redeemer

The principle of the protest was noble, but the cause did not justify the extremes. We went too far. The disc jockey's public apology should have sufficed. Perhaps, the offer of scholarship was not a bribe but a genuine apology that could have helped many students with their financial struggles. However, we just wanted our leaders to receive the respect they deserved.

After the protest, I was invited with the NOI student to fly to New York City for a television program. When we arrived at Laguardia Airport, we were transported by a more senior member of the NOI. After spending some time in this gentleman's home, we left for the television studio, meeting another NOI member on the way.

They knew that I was a Christian and we talked some. Yet, at the mention of Jesus, the driver put on a tape of Louis Farrakhan. He was addressing alleged contradictions in the genealogies of Christ in the accounts of Matthew and Luke. It was intriguing.

When I returned to Washington D.C., I was determined to hear the tape again. I went to a tape store and bought about twenty dollars worth of tapes by Louis Farrakhan. His eloquence was powerful. In desperation, I cried to the Lord, "If this is not true, please show me." Immediately, my tape recorder began to screech and reel very quickly. I rushed to it and turned it off. Then, I checked the tape and the tape recorder but found no defects. I sat for a few moments in shock.

I had only been a Christian for a few months. I thought to myself, "I've really done it this time. God is going to get me for being so gullible." I was like a child playing among snakes. I did not know the spiritual harm that my alliance had created for me. Scripture warns us against such coalitions, **"Do not be unequally yoked together with unbelievers . . ." (II Corinthians 6:14-16)** This does not mean that we should altogether avoid people with different beliefs. Such a stance is antithetical to the teachings of Christ, **"You are the salt of the earth but if the salt loses its saltiness, how can it be made salty again? It is no longer good for anything, except to be thrown out and trampled . . ." (Matthew 5:13)**

Salt must be mixed with meat for it to have a preserving effect. It must maintain its saltiness to be of any value. However, when a Christian puts himself in the position where his or her beliefs cannot be freely exercised, the very nature of the situation eliminates its purpose, **". . . to seek and**

God My Redeemer

save what was lost." (Luke 19:10)

In ignorance, I was walking contrary to scripture. This opened the door for the devil to attack my undeveloped faith. I was wrong but to Jesus I still belonged. A confused man in Chicago, with words greater than his understanding, was no match for the Lord of glory. Eloquence is no match for truth.

Islam

Islam was attractive only by default. Christ was disqualified because I considered some of the most vocal Christian leaders of that day to be racist. The Moral Majority was at its height and these were the same people who had condoned American apartheid. "God fearing" Christians of the South used dogs to bite innocent children. Fire hoses were turned on women and people were brutally beaten, all in the name of Christian conservatism.

I am a conservative in my view toward scripture but it would be unconscionable for me to become a part of the "religious right," as it is today. Notwithstanding, I am sometimes as opposed to the positions of the left wing, as I am toward the right. The born again experience and political conservatism are often presented as a package. This cheapens the blood of Christ. For me to become a conservative would have been like me selling my soul to the devil. Thus, to become born again was out of the question.

On the other side, to be a true liberal today would mean rejecting the teaching of Jesus. It is fundamentally wrong to declare that saving faith results in any strict political viewpoint, unless the position is clearly outlined in the scriptures.

As passionately as I might have felt about the racism in Christendom, converting to Islam would have been like jumping out of the frying pan into the fire. It was Arab Muslims who, "...contributed greatly to the development of the institution of slavery by seizing women for their harems and men for military and menial service."[1]

An African minister friend of mine commented that Islam is declining in parts of Africa while Christianity is surging. In America, among those who consider themselves afrocentric, the opposite trend is occurring. People are being duped.

The highly regarded Hadith, (the whole body of the sacred Traditions of the Muhammadans[2]) second only to the Koran in Islam

God My Redeemer

and essential reading for all those who want to understand this religion, refers to Mohammed as white.[3] Jesus is also portrayed as reddish-white.[4] Africans are often demeaned. In negative contexts, blacks are distinguished as having heads like raisins.[5] A dream of a black woman with uncombed hair was considered a bad omen.[6] In light of this, it would be dishonest to view racism as primarily a Christian phenomenon.

I have orthodox Muslim friends. They are people I love dearly. Although we socialize and care for each other, Islam and Christianity are incapable of synthesis. This is not because of some narrowness of our minds but honest evaluation. We respect each other but our faiths are divergent.

The Bible and Koran have irreconcilable differences, particularly when we compare the life and teaching of both men. Mohammed accepts the virgin birth but denies the crucifixion.[7] The crucifixion is an accepted historical fact. It is only the resurrection on which historians might debate. Furthermore, the Koran destines those who believe in the trinity to hell.[8]

Jesus teaches us to turn the other cheek in the face of religious persecution (Matthew 5:39). Mohammed teaches that Islam should advance

Out of Africa

through warfare.[9] Mohammed teaches that it is acceptable for men to beat their wives.[10] The scripture teaches the opposite that men are to honor their wives (I Peter 3:7). Mohammed married a six or seven-year-old girl named Aisha. He had sexual relations with her several years before she became a teenager.[11] Jesus never married and in spite of His thousands of female followers, He exploited no one. Additionally, the prophet's fifteen or more wives defied his own teaching.[12]

In almost every account where Jesus ministered to a woman, he violated social customs of the day and elevated her to a status that was revolutionary in His time (John 4:7-30; Matthew 9:20). We find the opposite in Islam. The Koran teaches that women are, ". . . deficient in intelligence and morality."[13] At times, the deranged have attempted to twist the Bible to justify attitudes such as Mohammed's but it is clearly contrary to the teaching of Jesus and sound Bible doctrine.

In Mohammed's era, his behavior might not have been so shocking. Nonetheless, it precludes his example from universal adherence. Yet, Jesus shines magnificently as the rock of ages. When we objectively compare the Mohammed of Islam with

God My Redeemer

the Jesus of scripture, there is no contest.

The Jesus the Bible reveals respected Africa. God chose that He spend some of His most formative years in Egypt (Matthew 2:13). Tradition states that Mark and Matthew were martyred in Africa.[14] If God thought that the lives of His own disciples were a fair wage for Africans to hear of the grace of our Savior, then no one can devalue the African.

Furthermore, Hamitic gentiles (descendants of Ham, the patriarch of all African peoples) are in Matthew's genealogy. Jesus was clearly Jewish, however, Jewish people are not always purely Semitic. Moses married an Ethiopian. Joseph married an Egyptian and fathered the Jewish tribes of Ephraim and Manasseh. Rahab, Ruth, and probably Bathsheba were also gentiles of Hamitic origin.

If Africans are morally and intellectually inferior because of race, then according to Matthew's genealogy, Jesus must be also. If this particular genealogy is a list of the family of Joseph and not Jesus, as some contend, then God selected a Jew with more Hamitic blood than others to be the stepfather of Jesus. God would not give Jesus an inferior step-father or mother.

Out of Africa

All the races of men probably have origins among dark people. Two white persons cannot have a brown child unless someone brown is in their ancestry. This is a fundamental genetic fact. The only logical conclusion one can arrive at is that the first man, Adam, was dark. Maybe, he had epicanthic, "Asian" eyelids. If this information is troubling and the reader feels hostile emotions, he should examine himself. Our emotions should not be invested in Adam's specific race. If they are, you should seek God's forgiveness.

DECEPTION

One of the most powerful instruments that Satan uses to oppress mankind are false religious systems. As Christians, we should be cautious but not afraid of deception. The primary function of the Spirit of Truth is to distinguish Himself from error. The Holy Ghost, if listened to and obeyed, is more than a match for any that would challenge His doctrine.

I heard a wonderful woman of God tell this story. One day, Truth undressed to go swimming. As he swam, Lie came along behind him and stole his clothes. After Lie put the clothes on, he walked toward a neighboring city. For several hours, he masqueraded as Truth.

God My Redeemer

However, just when Lie started feeling assured that his stunt had worked, the gatekeeper yelled, "Arrest that man!" The people asked, "Why?" He yelled back, "Because I can see the naked truth running toward the city!"

Deception had enveloped me but the Spirit of the Lord was still with me. His job was to ensure my spiritual liberty, that is, for me to know the truth and for the truth to set me free (John 8:32).

Satan had been making sport of me, very much like the bull that mistakenly charges the matador's cape. His real enemy is not the red cloth but the matador. Racism is merely a pretext through which the evil god of this world exploits his passions. Like many of my readers, I was a victim of this horrible device. Then entered Jesus and rescued me, like a burning stick snatched from the fire (Zechariah 3:2).

Gallantly, His grace arrested me. Through His shed blood at Calvary, He alone held the right to claim me. I can now boldly say, **"I know that my Redeemer lives."(Job 19:25)**

TWO

GOD WHO ORDAINS

My life had been dramatically changed. It was as if I had been standing between the rails of a train track, oblivious to the rhythm of the train wheels as they pulsated against the rail. The engine was approaching quickly. Suddenly, an arm swept me off the tracks. In a daze, I looked back at the tracks and saw the train whisk across where I had been standing. I then turned to the arm that grabbed me and saw that its owner was infinitely more imposing than the train.

Out of Africa

It is impossible not to be impressed by the character of the single most influential man in human history. Even if we do not understand and accept the message of Jesus, we must admire His manhood, brilliance, raw courage and impeccable integrity.

His Majesty submitted Himself to a human frame and became one of us. He obediently faced the worst of human brutality and won. He suffered in the Garden of Gethsemane because of Adam's sin in the Garden of Eden. He was nailed to a tree, in place of Adam, who wrongfully ate from a tree. Sin could not trap Him. Suffering could not crush Him. Satan could not hold Him.

He demonstrated further the love that compelled Him by taking from the tomb the fleshly vestige of His humanity. He wears it throughout glory as an eternal seal of His commitment to the redeemed. As the Father so loved the world that He gave us His only begotten Son, in like manner the nail scarred Christ desires to give the redeemed to our sin scarred world (John 3:16). After His resurrection, He said, **"As the Father has sent me, I am sending you." (John 20:21)**

As I connect the dots of my life, I notice a progression. God had saved me from sin but

God Who Ordains

likewise He had to call me into a righteous new purpose. Through two visions, Jesus would redirect my life with the same drama He first entered my life. God wanted to raise up a man of color without affiliation, accreditation or affirmation to prove that He could ordain and champion even one considered the least among us.

About one year after my conversion, Jesus appeared to me a second time. On this evening, as was my custom, I prepared to attend midweek services at my church but sensed the urging of the Holy Spirit to do otherwise. My girlfriend at that time, who was instrumental in leading me to Christ, went on to service and left me alone in her apartment.

Moments after she left, I sensed the presence of God in the room. His power seemed to emanate from behind me. When I turned to look, just above my head, I saw Jesus on the cross.

The Holy Spirit instantly burned in my heart a reverence for Christ that I had never known before. His suffering was clear. Yet, His pain on the cross was overshadowed by the reality of whom He was and is. The sublime was capsulized in a human frame and drank to the bitter dregs the frightful consequences of man's sin. All I wanted and could see was Him. He is much more than a mortal man. He was and is the immortal Christ, the Savior of the world. It is important for us to understand the suffering of our Savior. Yet, the cruelty of Calvary's altar was eclipsed by the presence of the sacrifice Himself, God taken on flesh. **"Blessed are the pure in heart, for they will see God." (Matthew 5:8)**

GO WHEREVER I LEAD YOU

The feeling of God's presence began to intensify in the room. Jesus said, "Stand up, close your eyes, bend over and go wherever I lead you." He was directing me as if I had a beam of the cross on my back - "**. . . If anyone would come after me, he must deny himself and take up his cross and follow me." (Matthew 16:24)**

He instructed me to walk quickly. I obeyed and walked head first wherever He led me. At one point, I became doubtful, thinking that God would never ask a person to do something as absurd as this. God quickly rebuked me for my lack of faith. Tears began to well in my eyes. I was frustrated that something so spiritual was happening but my mind was not validated with an explanation.

I did not like to be told what to do. Neither did I like the fact that He was always inside me

God Who Ordains

and did not seem to be governed by my reasoning. These feelings accompany every Christian until we learn the meaning of the saying, **"The mind set on the flesh is death, but the mind set on the Spirit is life and peace." (NAS Romans 8:6)** My attitude did not seem to affect Him at all. He just kept telling me where to walk. I completed my task without injury. This was a miracle in itself.

When my girlfriend returned to the apartment, she was very excited. I could see traces of tears on her cheeks. She asked me if anything had happened in the apartment while she was gone. I responded, "Jesus was here." She became even more excited and told me that while in the service, she saw both Jesus and me. She said He was standing above my head.

The Lord appeared to me on this occasion to prepare me for the many difficult days ahead. I would soon have to learn how to walk in his footsteps, by faith, in utter reliance on the Father. It was time for me to learn obedience. Jesus put it this way, **"If you love me, you will obey what I command." (John 14:15)** This truth is as faithful today as it was two thousand years ago.

Out of Africa

DO YOU LOVE ME?

Several months prior to this vision, the Holy Spirit said to me, "Simon bar Jonas, do you love me?" (Please read John 21:15-17) After a pause, He continued, "Feed my sheep." When He said it, I could not understand why He spoke this to me. Yet, His tone made it very clear that He was serious about this command.

I knew that God was calling me into the ministry. He would say things such as, "You will suffer many things for me." Other times, He would whisper, "I love you" into my spirit, as if I was going to experience something that could make me doubt it. This did not line up with what I wanted to believe.

Some preachers would mislead potential converts by telling them that if they follow Christ all their troubles will go away. The Bible teaches the opposite. In fact, ". . . **Everyone who wants to live a godly life in Christ will be persecuted." (II Timothy 3:12)** Perhaps, there would be less backsliding, if people were informed from the beginning that when we give our lives to Jesus, our trouble increases. However, if we trust Him, God will deliver and sustain us through it all. In the end, we will find that our greatest sacrifices do not even begin to compare with His ability to

God Who Ordains

reward us.

I was assured of God's call upon my life. What was repelling was the price of answering it. I knew that He wanted me to break off my relationship with my girlfriend. I loved her and intended to get married and live happily ever after. Finally, I obeyed. God loved us both and He knew what was best for our futures. Obviously, it was not each other. I had to choose between her and God.

Several days after I broke off the relationship, during my morning devotions, I sat down in my bedroom chair to listen to some music. As soon as I did so, it was as if a television screen was turned on inside me.

I stood up and went to turn off the music. On the way to my stereo, I closed and opened my eyes several times to see if the picture would go away. When I opened my eyes, I saw my natural surroundings. When I closed my eyes, I would see this scene. The colors were more beautiful than anything I had ever seen.

I questioned what I should do. In my heart, I knew that God was trying to tell me something. So I closed my eyes and got lost in the picture showing inside me.

THE BOAT

In the vision, I was seated in a fishing chair in the back of a boat. I was wearing my favorite summer hat. Various groups of people and a blue dog came running up my fishing line. I believe that the color blue represented the grace of God. The dog represented the members of a fraternity I had influenced for Christ. They were commonly referred to as "Q dogs." As the groups came into the boat, I opened the hull of the boat and they went in. All the people wore bright Hawaiian clothes. The clothes represented the free spirited college atmosphere that we all lived in.

Suddenly, a blue fish jumped out of the water, swallowed me and brought me to a dock. Jesus brought the boat to the shore. He was standing behind the steering wheel of the boat with a blue captain's hat on His head.

> **"For it became him, for whom are all things, and by whom are all things, in bringing many sons unto glory, to make the captain of their salvation perfect through sufferings." (KJV Hebrews 2:10)**

God Who Ordains

Jesus is in the business of bringing many sons to glory.

When He arrived at the dock, I remember pausing to stare at Him. It was as if time stopped. Without getting out of the boat, He said, "Let me show you how it was supposed to happen."

Instantly, the boat was back in the middle of the water. This time, instead of sticking the cargo into the hull of the ship, I was in the cabin tucking all my passengers into bed. God wanted me to become His servant and live a life that would provoke people to enter into his rest. **"Come to me, all you who are weary and burdened, and I will give you rest." (Matthew 11:28)**

Then, I saw Jesus walking above the water. At first, the flesh of His face was hard to see. His countenance seemed to fuse, yet from Him flowed a beauty that was consummate beyond words. His hair was not long and He did not appear to be taller than six feet. His robe fit Him well. He was not fat or skinny. He was perfect. He also had white feet. Later in the vision, He explained them this way, "Up till this time, the white man has carried my Gospel into the world, but this will change." Obviously, God was indicating that He planned to also use my black feet to help in His

Out of Africa

eternal plan.

People always want to know what color Jesus is. The truth of the matter is that He is the color of whatever house He lives in. If He lives in the reader's heart, He is the reader's color and shoe size. In this vision, He was my exact hue and color. Whether this is His actual color or He was just making a point to me, is not for discussion. What matters is that He made me understand that He is whatever race anyone that accepts Him is, ". . . **he who unites himself with the Lord is one with Him in spirit." (I Corinthians 6:17)**

While He was on the water, I asked him, "Lord, why did the fish swallow me up?" He stretched out His arm, and then pointed His finger at me. He said in the sternest voice I had ever heard, "Because you did not obey my word." I asked Him, "What word?" He said, "Feed my fish." He was clarifying His former command for me to feed His sheep.

As a child, I kept a fish tank. Every day, I would feed my fish. These tropical fish were helpless. Without my care, they would die.

After He told me to feed His fish, I asked myself on the inside, "Why didn't I do it?" The

God Who Ordains

Lord must have overheard my thought because He said in a piercing tone, "Because of hate, doubt and fear."

I asked Him, "Who do I hate?" I thought He was going to say white people because I was concentrating on His white feet, which did not match the rest of His body. His response was quite the contrary. He said, "Yourself." His answer dumbfounded me. If I did not receive a reverential fear of God the time He appeared to me on the cross, I certainly received it then. Like the disciples on different occasions, I was too afraid to ask Him anything else (Mark 9:32).

My boat arrived at the dock. I gave the people a hand as they stepped down off the boat. Then the Lord said, "You are on the shore of the apostles and prophets." Finally, when all of my passengers left, a girl returned and put what appeared to be a Hawaiian lei around my neck but was in fact a harness. Marriage was often spoken of as a yoke in Bible days. God was promising me that I would one day be married. After she left, the scene disappeared.

All that remained was the sound of footsteps in my belly and then I saw the Lord again. He uttered these final words to me, "This is where I'll always be." God lives in our most inward parts.

THE SHORE

In John 21:4 the Bible says, ". . . **Jesus stood on the shore.**" Jesus could have appeared to His disciples on the ship. He could have even appeared to them on the water. Either of these places would have been more convenient for His disciples.

Why did Jesus stand on the shore? Because the shore is where the disciples should have been. Peter and the other disciples had no business on the sea. Jesus had called them to be fishers of men, not fish. This job can only be done on dry land.

Like Peter, I had a boat. The boat in my vision represented my old way of life. On it, I had my old friends, even the woman I had intended to marry. If I was going to answer the call of God upon my life, I needed to get to my shore - the shore of the apostles and prophets. I had to follow Him in like faith of the ancients.

Of course, there are not apostles or prophets in the same category today as the twelve disciples or those who were moved upon to write scripture.

God Who Ordains

Modern apostles are simply missionaries, men and women given an unusual commission. Contemporary prophets are simply those called as spokespeople for specific truths.

In some circles, everyone is calling themselves an apostle or prophet. I use these terms with caution. They are biblical terms but they can imply much more in our society than my intended usage.

In this vision, I was being warned. I had two choices. I could come to the shore with ease or through tribulation. Like Jonah, either a fish would take me to shore or I could willingly kiss good night those I loved, to whom eventually I would have to say goodbye, and come to the shore.

WHY DIDN'T I DO IT?

I often tell people that the greatest challenge they are going to face in life is not the devil, but themselves. In the vision, I asked myself, "Why didn't I do it?" Why didn't I obey God's word to feed His fish? According to the Lord, my problem was not directly with the devil but with my own self-hatred, doubts and fears. Conquering these thieves of our lives' potential is what faith is all about.

Out of Africa

Weeks later, to confirm this vision, the Spirit of God moved on my heart again. While walking across campus, a friend and I began to talk about the faith of Abraham. We talked particularly about how Abraham was willing to leave his home to go into a foreign land, simply because a God he barely knew had told him to do so. At the end of our discussion, the Holy Spirit asked me if I would do the same.

In the pit of my stomach, I began to feel that I would never return to Howard University again. This thought troubled me. God intended for me to return but in a different capacity, not as a student but as a minister.

It was much easier to talk about the faith of Abraham than to produce such faith for myself. I was in my senior year. The thought of not completing my education after I had come so far was absurd. The unreasonable nature of God's leading aggravated me. It seemed that He wanted to make a fool of me. Please note: God is not against education. Pursuing a degree is a noble pursuit. However, for reasons that are perhaps in the category of "secret things," (Deuteronomy 29:29) God wanted to train me outside of an institution.

God Who Ordains

Days later, I was alone in my bedroom and the presence of the Lord filled the room. The Holy Spirit spoke these life changing words to my heart, "Let no school say it trained you, let no man say he made you rich and let no woman say she is your reward."

These were the loneliest words I had ever heard God speak to me. After he spoke, I laid down on my bed in grief. I thought, how could a person with so much inner turmoil, expect to succeed at believing God? I was convinced that my doubts would cause God to eventually reject me and leave me with nothing.

A few moments later, I sensed the presence of the Lord again. The Holy Spirit began to brood over me. He seemed to have a maternal affection for me. I could not accept this. I had assumed that the Holy Spirit was purely male. His cry for my spiritual dependency was counter to what I thought was "macho." I was an independent, self sufficient, and somewhat hardened young man and I did not readily understand His call for my dependence. My father is a veteran of the Korean War and a product of the South Bronx. I thought men should have a tighter rein on their sensitivities. God was obviously falling short of my ideals.

Out of Africa

In spite of my immaturity, God allowed me to see into His heart. I did not realize that God experienced such intense feelings. This is not to say that His emotions are a ruling part of His nature, but He definitely has feelings. If He ever attempted to distort His true feelings, He would be a liar, like many of us men. We should never deny that we have feelings, we just should not allow our passions to overrule our principles. When Christ faced His midnight hour, He said, ". . . **My soul is overwhelmed with sorrow to the point of death. Stay here and keep watch with me." Matthew 26:38)**

Things seemed to be happening so fast and spiritual things were still new to me. I wanted to wait a few years, until I had a greater assurance that I could successfully do what God was asking. However, there is nothing more sure than God's Word. I just needed to step out and walk on it. Dr. King once said:

> "Cowardice asks the question, 'Is it safe?' Expedience asks the question, 'Is it politic?' Vanity asks the question, 'Is it popular?' But conscience asks that question, 'Is it right?' And there comes a time when one must take a position that is

God My Sanctifier

we cling to Jesus in precious faith, right behavior will be a natural outcome. Yet, if we decide not to obey God in some area of our lives, it will be only a matter of time before our independence manifests itself in more concrete and immoral terms.

I had no intention to do as the Lord had told me: "Let no school say it trained you, let no man say he made you rich and let no woman say she is your reward." I did not plan to leave school and enter the ministry. I did not plan to allow God to provide for me apart from the career path that I was traveling. Lastly, although celibate, at times I felt like giving up my life of holiness for the fleeting pleasures of sin.

In the fall of 1987, I was convinced by some friends to interview for a cooperative internship with a major corporation in New York. I got the job and left D.C. in July. I continued to pray, read the Bible and found a church in New York but in spite of all my religiosity, the next seven months were some of the most miserable months of my life.

In January of the following year, when I had finished my internship, I returned to Washington, D.C. Instead of getting another job in my field, a job opened up for me working with gifted kids.

Out of Africa

Before long, I was promoted into the business side of the organization and loved it.

I enrolled in summer school and after work, I attended class to retake the math course I had failed. I failed it again. In the fall, I registered in the course again. By then, the job that was once going so well, turned so sour that I resigned.

While at this job, my heart ached so much that I felt like crying most of the work day. I was convinced that God did not love me. My mind could not fathom the terrible thing that I had done that would cause me such unrest. After all, I was a churchgoer and was abstinent. What more could God want? All this Abraham stuff was silly to me.

I completed the math course again in the fall. I was so sure that I had failed; I did not even look to see the posting of my final grade. Math had always been a difficult subject for me. However, I had passed business courses that required higher math skills than the math course I had consistently failed.

My problem passing the math course was mystical to me. One day, while I was musing the situation, God spoke to me. He said, "I resist the proud and I resist you down in there (speaking of

God My Sanctifier

my spirit, which is the seat of our minds, will and emotions)." It was hard for me to believe that God was that tough. Jesus did not intend to lose His fight with me. He was intent on teaching me which one of us was boss, even if it took Him a few years. The new birth alone does not guarantee success. Success is promised only to the willing and obedient (Isaiah 1:19).

Finally, after sitting in the class for at least five semesters, I gave up and decided that there was no way I was going to pass the math sequence of my business major. This stubbornness of mine, God wanted to redirect and one day use for His glory. I went to a friend for advice. He said that God wanted me to study philosophy because of my analytical strengths. (We should be careful about lightly giving advice in the name of God) I foolishly agreed.

I was fighting with God with all my might. He was not going to win by default. The battle of our wills would not end until He was clearly proven the strongest. Why would a man resist God?

In the Spring session of 1988, I enrolled in philosophy. When I opened my book to study Kant, Plato, Locke and others, it was terrible.

Out of Africa

Their vanity dripped from the pages. This is not to say that God cannot grace a Christian to study philosophy. It was just something that I should not have done outside of His will.

Sometimes my spirit would feel so grieved, I found myself not being able to study for my tests. I tried my best to rid myself of this nagging presence in my inner man. The Holy Spirit would not back down. I was testing God's resolve and He passed with flying colors.

Finally, I just gave up and quit. I dropped out of school. My family thought I was having a mental breakdown. It had become difficult for me to keep a steady job. I went from being someone presumably headed for success, who had been in local newspapers, on television and radio, and who for a couple editions had his own column in the campus newspaper, to what some considered a total failure.

I sat in meetings with some of the most famous African Americans alive at that time. I went from life's fast track to waiting tables and attempting to sell encyclopedias. Finally, I became a bellman at a hotel forty minutes from where I lived. I had to wake up at 4:00 a.m. just to get to work on time.

God My Sanctifier

Jesus was winning the fight! My last bastion in the fight for independence was in the fact that I could still be a "good person," without going overboard and becoming a preacher. My morality was obnoxious in the sight of God. There is no righteousness without obedience to and abiding in the will of God for our lives.

CLAY FEET

Sex, money and reputation are the primary areas where Satan would like to gain advantage in the life of the believer. As I resisted the will of God for my life, all of these areas began to ripen for the tempter's harvest.

At the hotel where I worked, one of my managers was a young lady whom I had lived with the summer before I became a Christian. When we lived together, I had the more promising job and made more money. By this time, the tables had dramatically turned. This challenged my masculine pride.

One morning, I decided that life without God would be easier than life with Him. I told God that I was tired and that I was not going to resist the devil any longer. By this time, I had been a Christian for three years. From the time I first understood what the Bible outlines as God's

Out of Africa

plan for our sexuality, I had been faithful to obey. This was maybe the single most convincing proof of my conversion to those who knew me.

By the time night fell, I had made the phone call, bought a bottle of wine and was spending the night with my ex-girlfriend/roommate. However, the wine was not strong enough. All through the experience, I felt a distracting compassion for her soul. Having sex with a wounded conscience is absurd. The pleasure is swallowed up by the conviction. On the outside, I may have looked like the same boy she had known years ago but on the inside, I was a totally new person. I began to realize for the first time how real my new birth in Christ was.

I was not the same boy who had relations with her in the past. I felt disgraced by my actions. I did not love her the way one who would share such an intimate experience with her should. After walking with Jesus, sex had become sacred to me. In my estimation, I had violated and made contemptible one of the most beautiful gifts God has given men and women to share. I felt like slime.

Scripture does not command that we live pure lives because God is an ogre. He simply

God My Sanctifier

wants to protect us. Our emotions, bodies and progeny are so precious in His sight that He does not condone sexual relations outside the berth of a covenant relationship. Only when a man is willing to lay down his life for his woman and is willing to publicly and in the sight of God, give himself exclusively to his bride in marriage, does a woman find a setting dignified enough for her to offer to him the most intimate parts of her body. The emotional bond that develops between two healthy people during intercourse was not created to be broken. May God forgive and heal us of our folly.

REBOUND

I immediately quit my job and began to fast until my pants began to fall off. I was desperate for God's help. Finally, I began to realize that the only way I could be an honorable man was to honor God's will for my life. I had to devote myself spirit, soul and body to a heavenly mission.

It was during this time that God placed his anointing on me and told me, "Cease from your works and do my works." (Hebrews 4:10) After weeks of prayer and fasting, I was invited to my first preaching engagement in Pittsburgh, Pennsylvania. Shortly, thereafter, I became a leader in the campus ministry in which I had met the Lord.

Out of Africa

This was a tragic time in my life. Out of tragedy, God intended to bring triumph. God still had a plan for me. He loved me and I still loved Him. Every step I took to sanctify myself to His purposes, He responded to by showing me that nothing could separate me from His love.

The most important thing that this situation taught me and the reader would do well to learn, is that God never intended our right living to be just the result of a strong will. If that is the case, we should celebrate our volition as much as God's grace. Right living is to be the result of a right relationship with the Father. If I do what is good, it is only the result of my relationship with my Creator. If I do what is wrong, it is because at some point, I hid myself from His cleansing presence. Lord, continue to set us apart from sin as You draw us nearer to You.

FOUR

GOD MY VINDICATOR

One day, the Sun commissioned an artist to draw his likeness. The next morning, the artist arose at sunrise to start the project. He spent all morning and afternoon completing what he thought was an exact portrait. In the evening, he presented his work to the Sun. The Sun rejected the portrait.

For weeks, things went on this way. Finally, the artist grew frustrated and decided not to arise at dawn to paint the Sun. As the morning began to pass, the Sun crept into his room, through the

Out of Africa

blinds of his window, just above the head of his bed. As the Sun's warmth began to caress his skin, he awoke. While wiping the sleep from his eyes, he heard the birds singing and the children playing. Then it dawned on the young man - the Sun's beauty is not his sunrise or sunset. The greatest beauty of the Sun is seen in the life it sustains.

Scripture says that, **"Charm is deceptive, and beauty is fleeting; . . ."(Proverbs 31:30)** The Sun's true beauty was not its brilliant rays but its light and warmth. The measure of our Christianity does not rest on our charismatic experience or exegetical skills but the fruit of our everyday living. Are we just flashes in the sky or in times of darkness, are we a light? When the winds of life are bitter, do people feel our inner warmth?

I was redeemed through the blood of Jesus. I was ordained by the very mouth of Jesus. I had been sanctified by the Spirit of Christ but would I remain true when faced with a cardinal reality of Christianity,

> **"Bless those who persecute you; bless and do not curse . . . Do not take revenge, my friends, but leave room for God's wrath, for it is**

God My Vindicator

written it is mine to avenge; I will repay, says the Lord."(Romans 12:14 & 19)

I was shining like the sun but would my "New York temper" consume my light and warmth? Was I big enough not to take matters in my own hands and let God be my vindicator?

I had now been in full-time ministry at Howard University for one year. I had become very discouraged. My clothes were old. Some of my bills were behind and I had spent days hungry. I felt that my prayers were taking too long getting answered.

I subconsciously began to provoke God. I knew God wanted me to stay in ministry in Washington D.C. Yet, I reasoned that I was unprepared for ministry and needed more formal training, in spite of His earlier instruction, "Let no school say it trained you . . ."

I planned to leave for Bible school the following fall. My pastor and chaplain agreed and I announced to my students that I would leave for Oklahoma. By the way, during this time, God really did tell me to go to Oklahoma. That summer, I attended my first camp meeting there.

Out of Africa

Obviously, I had overstated God's intention for me.

Several days after my announcement, I awoke and as my custom was, I prepared to go to the grocery store to buy my breakfast. Instead of driving as I normally did, I walked to the store. I suppose God wanted me to eat breakfast before I had the opportunity to lose my appetite.

After breakfast, I walked toward my car to run my errands for the day. As I approached the car, a frantic woman greeted me. She told me that the car next to her own had been vandalized. As I walked up the hill to where my car was parked, the first thing I saw was my smashed front windshield and a foul statement, in large letters, scratched in brick across the hood.

I paused in amazement. It looked like a wild man had attacked my car. The rear window was smashed. The paint on the sides of my car was scratched and glass covered the inside of the automobile. In addition to this, I found that the assailants had entered the car and poked a hole through the roof. Weird!

I kept cool. However, I immediately knew in my spirit who was responsible. It was hard for

God My Vindicator

my head to accept that a Christian was capable of such an act. The Bible teaches that the flesh of man is corrupt. If we yield ourselves to it, we will certainly be the instruments of sin (Romans 6:13).

My first thought was, "Why didn't God wake me last night so that I could come out here to stop this?" The answer to this question was obvious. Upon recognizing the culprits, it would have required more restraint than I would have wanted to use. To settle a matter with my hands was not at all foreign to me. Yet, I do not believe that God wanted me to preach from a prison cell.

CAIN

³In the course of time Cain brought some of the fruits of the soil as an offering to the Lord.

⁴But Able brought fat portions from some of the firstborn of his flock. The Lord looked with favor on Able and his offering,

⁵But on Cain and his offering he did not look with favor. So Cain was very angry, and his face was downcast.

⁶Then the Lord said to Cain, "Why are you angry? Why is your face downcast?

Out of Africa

⁷If you do what is right, will you not be accepted? But if you do not do what is right, sin is crouching at your door; it desires to have you, but you must master it."
⁸Now Cain said to his brother Able, "Let's go out to the field." And while they were in the field, Cain attacked his brother Able and killed him. (Genesis 4:3-8)

The person who led in the assault was at one time my best friend and a leader in the ministry of which I was a part. We knocked on many dormitory doors together, walked up and down streets together, spreading the Good News of Jesus Christ with results. We spent countless hours of prayer and hung out together. I still love the brother, in Christ.

I had never knowingly wronged this person. The only possible motivation for his action was a jealousy that had grown to fruit-bearing proportions. In my mind, I could hear God speaking into this young man's life across time, **"Then the Lord said to Cain, 'Why are you angry? Why is your face downcast? If you do what is right, will you not be accepted? . . .' "(Genesis 4:6-7)** In other words, God said, "No

God My Vindicator

need to be jealous, just do right and I will reward you?" Some need to stop spending so much time thinking about their brothers' and sisters' affairs and use that same energy to follow God for themselves.

Why did Cain want to kill Abel? He wanted to kill him because Abel's good deeds were a witness against Cain. When you decide to walk before the Lord, those who refuse to live likewise are going to hate you. Why? Because you represent what they have failed to obtain. Your success eliminates their excuses for why they do not try. Jesus states this reality in Matthew 5:11: **"Blessed are you when people insult you, persecute you and falsely say all kinds of evil against you because of me."** In other words, some people will revile, persecute and say all manner of evil against you, if you let God bless you. Let Him bless you anyway. It is worth the persecution.

If we are going to truly be witnesses for God, we must be prepared to deal with the wrath of the "brotherhood." Every person who has endeavored to follow God has been hated, misunderstood and demonized by their opponents. True Christianity is the commitment to do anything and everything God requires, regardless of the consequences.

NAME CALLING

After my car was vandalized, my closest friend and the greater portion of my ministry began to call me names. The person who had done the vandalism began to start his own ministry of spreading accusations against me. Those who did the name calling were some of the ones to whom I had given my last dollars, and prayed for late into the night.

The closeness of our past association was the basis he used to establish his authority as a qualified judge of my character. Such a premise could also justify the betrayal of Judas. We need to be more thoughtful when we hear rumors about our brothers and sisters.

Shortly after the incident, I canceled my plans to go to Bible school. When I committed to stay, God told me to announce to the members of the fellowship, who had vandalized my vehicle. When I named the culprit, my ex-roommate denied the charges. Most of the ministry's participants sided with him, concluding that my position had made me cocky, to the degree that I would make up false charges against one of the brethren, simply based on my personal suspicions.

God My Vindicator

They felt that I was taking too much upon myself to announce whom God had told me vandalized my car, without other forms of proof. God does not usually speak to me about such issues but when He does, I need to have the guts to say so. If time had proven me wrong, I would have apologized and done all that I could to make things right.

As time passed, I began to second guess myself and thought that maybe I was wrong. I attempted to reconcile the matter with my accuser. Before this time, if he saw me, he and other ex-members of the ministry would cross to the other side of the street. If I happened to see him and nobody else was around when I greeted him, he would ignore me. If he saw me and someone he felt was sympathetic to me, my greeting to him was followed by a hello. Since we had common friends, it was difficult not to see him. My biggest challenge was not "beating his brains out."

Finally, I got a chance to talk with him and attempted to settle the matter. In this conversation, he told me that his heart was broken when he heard of the damage done to my automobile. He said that he had great respect for me. Yet, after the conversation, he continued to tell almost everyone who had anything to do with me, how I had falsely accused him and had gone off the deep end. I could not think of anything that I could do to fix the problem, so I tried my best to just forget about it.

ZERO HOUR

In the fall of the following year, the fall out from this incident was so great, we were faced with practically starting the ministry all over again. In spite of this, we began to grow. However, my old friends who had become my new enemies, incessantly sowed seeds of discord among the ministry's newer participants.

Several months after the car incident, God began to deal with me about planting my first church. After preaching to hundreds, Song of Faith Church began with a congregation of only six people.

The problems at campus affected my Sunday morning meetings drastically. For many months, I led my faithful six and sometimes seven. Eventually, more and more people began to visit on Sunday mornings. However, without fail, the disgruntled people of the past would make it a point to get hold of the newcomers and suggest all manner of evil against me.

God My Vindicator

There was never a solid character or doctrinal flaw that was pointed out that merited such opposition. Innuendo had been the key tool used to discourage potential church members. This form of manipulation is common and the worst part of religious life. Fact and not suspicion is the basis on which we should assert truth.

What baffled me most about my opponents was that I had often laid my hands on their heads and prophesied into their lives words of wisdom and knowledge, only God could reveal. Not one of the words I had spoken into any of their lives ever fell to the ground. They all came to pass.

GOD HELP!

Finally, I got fed up. I prayed to God and said, "I am not your apostle, if you let this continue. God, you are just going to have to get another boy. I am not an apostle." He told me afterwards that he was pleased with my prayer. One might think I was out of line to pray this way but I was acting as a missionary to that campus and wanted God to honor my work as such. If things continued as they were, I could not be an effective soul winner.

When Sunday came around, I preached from II Kings 1:10: ". . . **If I am a man of God, may**

Out of Africa

fire come down from heaven . . ." After that message, God told me that He was delivering my enemies over to the devil. Within two weeks, things got bizarre. The person whom God had told me attacked my car, began making menacing, anonymous phone calls to his posse, cursing them and threatening one of their lives. He tried to muffle his voice, but it was recognized.

Surprisingly, I was asked for counsel on the matter. The anger of the person he threatened caused her to confess to me. He had told her and one other that he had vandalized my car. As news got around, they began to turn on each other. As shocking as this may sound, black on black crime is rampant on the streets because it is so prevalent in the Church. Before we can stop the trouble on the streets, this must be stopped in the Church. **"For it is time for judgment to begin with the family of God;. . ."(I Peter 4:17)**

Days after my automobile was vandalized, I consulted my African American pastor about it. He actually seemed pleased at my misfortune. Further, a mutual friend and an Elder in the church, who had been a father figure to many of us, told me that he would rather have his genitals (politely stated for the reader) cut off than to believe me.

God My Vindicator

Both men had been personally involved in my ministry at campus. Unfortunately, they did not have a paternal concern for me. They did not view me as a son but as their potential competition. Black men, we must stop this!

After the guy confessed, I made it a point to call this Elder, hoping to mend the bridge. He did not show any sense of remorse and by that time, I did not belong to that church, so my friendship was of no value. He simply excused the behavior of the other young man, who was still a member.

Only one person immediately apologized to me. Since then, I have seen many of their lives take horrible turns. God's judgment is not always swift but it is certain against those who refuse to follow Him, by walking in love. Our enemies may seem to prosper but in the end they will be cut down (Psalms 37:1-2). For this reason, we pray that our enemies see the error of their way.

The proverb given by Jesus is true,". . . **Only in his hometown and in his own house (family) is a prophet without honor." (Matthew 13:57)** We have loved those the dearest that show us the greatest disrespect. Those whom we feel should be the most accepting of God's hand in our lives, are often the most rejecting of it. In spite of this fact, **"When a man's ways are pleasing to the Lord, he makes even his enemies live at peace with him." (Proverbs 16:7)**

The greatest obstacle we have dealing with personal rejection is keeping our emotions under control. Emotions are sometimes selfish and irrational. If not managed properly, they can be the downfall of any person who walks by faith. This was not easy. Yet during these times, I believed in my heart that if I was faithful to do the best I could to manifest the character of Jesus, it would not be too long before God would manifest His power on my behalf.

Apart from God, a minister has only one thing to rely on - his reputation. Usually, if this is tarnished, the minister is ruined. Some nights, it felt like my emotions were overcoming my mind. These people were not attacking my hobby, but my life's commitment.

I would sometimes with clenched teeth, feel tears fall from my eyes, as I went to sleep. What was most painful is that God did not do anything to stop them. He said to me one day, "Derek, I cannot stop your pain. All I can do is make it up to you." **"I consider that our present sufferings are not worth comparing with the glory that**

God My Vindicator

will be revealed in us." (Romans 8:18)

Because I would come to Him with my hurts, every tear I shed was used to purge my emotions from the damaging effects of resentment. If we cried fewer tears of self-pity and more out of an utter determination to please God, we would begin to truly touch and experience the compassionate nature of our High Priest, Jesus.

Often, God allows times of public humiliation before His greatest works of exaltation, in the lives of His people. It is like learning to ride a bike. The teacher must allow our undeveloped sense of balance to face the challenge of a bumpy road and the possibility of falling, before we can master the sport.

I have learned that when we feel overwhelmed, if we first take our problem to God in prayer, He will prove to be our vindicator. He does not necessarily exonerate us by causing mishap in the lives of our enemies. That's the devil's job. God just ensures that in the process of time, the specious claims against us will be proven false.

As with the crucifixion and resurrection of Jesus, He will reach down into our darkest hour

Out of Africa

and blow back into our lives, the quickening breath of life. We would have gained more than mere head knowledge; we would have personally experienced His saving power. The darkest hour is just before the dawn. Weeping may remain for a night, but vindication comes in the morning (Psalms 30:5). All God wants is for us to stay true to Him until the morning comes.

FIVE

GOD MY BANNER

During the War of 1812, the British navy attacked Ft. McHenry in Baltimore, Maryland. The British fleet was the most feared navy in the world. America was a young nation and this war was a test of our resolve against European expansionism.

On September 13, 1814, the British navy attacked the American port. Through that night, Francis Scott Key heard the bombs bursting in the air and saw the rocket's red glare, with great

Out of Africa

apprehension. When morning dawned, he looked to see if the fort had been captured. When he had enough light to see into the distance, he saw the red, white and blue banner still waving. At the sight, he knew the British had not prevailed. These events inspired him to write a poem that would later become our national anthem, *The Star Spangled Banner*.

I suppose that this story could have made a greater hero out of Francis Scott Key, if he had slept and awoke holding an unshakable confidence in the endurance of the United States armed forces. However, the most beautiful poetry is often written only when our hopes survive our fears.

Like Francis Scott Key, I have had many apprehensive moments straining to see if the banner of righteousness was still waving. Could my ideals withstand an institution? Could a young man believe God and that be enough?

About one year before I entered full-time ministry, I became friends with a university chaplain. He was very poor and quite unhappy. Nonetheless, I felt that his intentions were noble, so I took it upon myself to aid him.

Whenever he had a meeting, I would attend.

God My Banner

If he needed help of any kind, I would volunteer. We prayed together. After a while, we even began to pitch in to eat together. Brothers we should support one another.

He was affiliated with an organization that he felt was not adequately providing for him. On occasion, when I knew his needs were great, I would give him my whole paycheck, as an offering to God. Instead of him having to believe God for his bills to be paid, I would believe God for mine. I felt that this was the type of brotherhood that Christ called for in His Church.

When I began to financially assist this man, I did not realize that I was sowing seeds for my own future. At the time, I was not aware of it but through our friendship, God was preparing me to also face the challenges of ministry. Only one year later, I entered full-time ministry.

After my first preaching engagement, this campus minister's co-coordinator quit. God spoke to my heart to fill the position. When I talked to him about it, he believed that it was God's will for me to take on this new role. I felt honored.

During most of the summer, I led the student prayer group, which I had already

Out of Africa

participated in for about a year and a half, under his leadership. By the beginning of the school year, he had me doing most of the preaching. The numbers in the ministry began to increase sharply. A small revival had started.

By Christmas, I quit. The relationship between the two of us had become very strained. The student's response to my preaching had exceeded his own and this made things difficult. Our rapport was too high a price for me to pay for preaching. I did not think I preached well and this was just the kind of excuse that I was looking for so that I could give it up.

The next semester, services were started without my participation. However, the meetings were not going very well, so I returned and the ministry continued to grow.

Soon, I was introduced to the workings of religious politics. I began to see that financial concerns were motivating the decisions of the ministry. This was very hard for me to accept. If God has called us to serve Him, we should not have to compromise for Him to provide for us. I would follow whatever decision my senior made but it was often with objections.

God My Banner

By the following summer, he felt impressed of the Holy Spirit that I should begin to lead the ministry and that he should have a secondary role. The year had been very difficult for me. I did not want to continue in the ministry. In my mind, leading the ministry was out of the question.

After a few days, I went to him and apologized for allowing things to become so uncomfortable between us that he would forfeit his position. I asked him to remain the head of the ministry. Obviously, I could not believe that God wanted me to have such responsibility.

When school started in the fall, he continued to have the supervising role. I was responsible for the oversight of the spiritual aspects of the ministry - prayer, counseling and preaching. His primary task was to take care of the business side of things. Ministers with financial commitments to my senior were invited to teach, although they had conflicting commitments to the Word. This was a great problem for us.

The money received from outside sources went to his salary. Thus, he needed to have certain ministers speak at our meetings. I had never been supported by an outside ministry. Moreover, at times, I chose to lose weight rather than make a

Out of Africa

deal of some sort. It may sound prideful for me not to have sought outside ministries for support. However, it is important to understand that the integrity of God's call upon my life needed to have been tested and proven before I could have the confidence that I have today.

My faith was fixed. If God called me, He would also have to provide for me. It is not wrong to accept money from an outside group. I just was not willing to jump through the many proverbial hoops often attached to such support.

I had studied sales in business school. I felt that a man of God should not have to market himself to the Church like a new deodorant or shampoo. I believe that the man of God's primary focus should be prayer, the study of the Word, loving God's people and obeying the voice of the Lord. I know what I just wrote offended a few preachers. I am not saying that we should not take offerings. I am simply saying that we should not sacrifice our integrity for financial gain.

By the second school year, I had learned that God would not let me just quit. Yet, I could not continue in my capacity with the tension that existed between myself and my senior. It was a very difficult situation.

God My Banner

MISGUIDED

I began kicking myself for bucking practices that I probably had no power to change. I tried to be as innocuous as possible. This was as unnatural as a dog trying to meow.

I was in the predicament of Jeremiah, **"But if I say, 'I will not mention him or speak any more in his name,' his word is in my heart like a fire, a fire shut in my bones. I weary of holding it in; indeed, I cannot."** (Jeremiah 20:9) I would try to be nice but invariably, the power of God would come upon me and I would upset everything.

I finally got fed up. I began to pray consistently about the matter. The Holy Spirit began to convict me of not accepting the leadership of the ministry when He first moved upon the chaplain to give it to me. I shared this with my senior and without argument, he agreed to submit. However, when there arose a disagreement between the two of us, he would 'pull rank,' as if he was still the senior in the relationship. More times than not, I felt beholden to allow this because he was older.

As Christmas approached, I told him that I would quit if he did not formally give me charge

Out of Africa

of the ministry. I did not say that I would destroy the ministry or start my own. I simply told him that I would quit. When he felt that I was serious about the threat, he agreed. Immediately, I changed the name and mission of the fellowship. The wisdom of Jesus spoke to this situation.

> "^{36}**No one tears a patch from a new garment and sews it on an old one. If he does, he will have torn the new garment, and the patch from the new will not match the old.**
> ^{37}**And no one pours new wine into old wineskins. If he does, the new wine will burst the skins. The wine will run out and the wineskins will be ruined.**
> ^{38}**No, new wine must be poured into new wineskins." (Luke 5:36-38)**

BEWARE OF DOGS

Shortly, thereafter, I was treading the waters of a major controversy. I had posted a flier that had a picture of a sign with the statement, "Beware of Dogs." Beneath the sign was the scripture reference for Philippians 3:2. Also, on the flier was the statement, "Allah is not God,

God My Banner

Mohammed is Dead" and the time and dates that I would preach on these issues. The language on this flier was consistent with the language of many fliers commonly distributed at Howard University.

The fliers caused such a stir that the administration closed the meeting place for fear of a riot. I preached anyway but outside, face to face with angry protesters. The sermon addressed the doctrine of the Nation of Islam (NOI) that declared black men to be gods and white people, devils. From this time on, we were told that I was "persona non grata" at Howard University. I spent thousands of dollars to attend this school. I had spent two years serving the Christian students on that campus and for a flier many times less incendiary than other rhetoric preached and advertised on that campus, I was unwelcome. When sanity is so suspended, we can be sure that demons are involved.

During this period, the Lord appeared to me again. He was standing up but there was nothing visible under his feet. All He said was, "Stand on my word." He was referring to what He had told me shortly after I began in the ministry. He said to me, "Teach my people to follow my voice, preach my soon return and prophesy against iniquity. The last one will get you into trouble." His word was

Out of Africa

being fulfilled. I was in a lot of trouble.

Years have passed since this incident. The NOI has since gained prominence as one of the most powerful forces in the African American community. Although, this may put me at odds with many, I still say, **"Watch out for those dogs, those men who do evil, those mutilators of the flesh." (Philippians 3:2)**

Philippians 3:2 addressed people who trusted in circumcision, a physical factor, to establish their righteousness. Neither the whiteness of the members of the skinheads nor the color of the NOI supporters makes either group righteous. Righteousness is the result of faith, not race.

This flier also offended orthodox Muslims. If I was intentionally addressing that community, the flier would have been far less abrasive. Nonetheless, the Bible teaches that Mohammed is not a true prophet and I should have the freedom to say so without my life being threatened. It would be unthinkable to threaten a Muslim because he does not believe in the deity and blood atonement of Jesus Christ. Likewise, I should have the liberty to express my convictions.

One would think such a position would be

applauded by so-called Christian leaders. To the contrary, I was blasted by scholars and religious leaders at the University. Perhaps they never read that Mohammed likened Jews to jackasses[1] or that Jesus likened the leaders of His day to foxes (Luke 13:32) and snakes (Matthew 12:34). In this same tradition, I used an analogy to illustrate a truth.

Moreover, the man whom I had supported throughout the years, my mentor, turned his back on me. When I first heard the call to start Song of Faith Church, we had several meetings discussing his participation in forming this new church. When the church was started, he never even visited and soon had enough momentum from my fall out with the administration to begin telling people that I was a fraud.

I was labeled a, "true believer." Although it was sown to discredit me, it actually honored me. I pray that we could all be true believers. As persecution caused the early Christians to finally leave Israel and begin to evangelize the world, circumstances were pushing me where God had called me to. God used it all to His glory.

A BODY OF DEATH

No human being on earth has arrived at a state of perfection. Even the Apostle Paul

Out of Africa

admitted, "Not that I have already obtained all this, or have already been made perfect, but I press on to take hold of that for which Christ Jesus took hold of me." (Philippians 3:12)

Every person, until we receive our glorified bodies, has an opaque island, full of ebony trees and caverns paved with onyx stones. The sand is black and the sky is lowering. Yet, the waters are as clear as the finest crystal. The sea beats the shore with a constant rhythm that calls to the deepest streams of our being.

To answer the summons of the sea, we must leave the darkness of our pasts and muster the courage to dive from our piers of disillusionment, into the pure flow of divine supply. As we journey from the shore, invariably, we will begin to tire and sink. This is not the time to turn back. To swim as God intended, we must first drown in the unrelenting sea of His love.

As we gasp for air and the waters of life begin to conquer our souls, we will begin to discover our fins and gills. The breath we once required from the vapor is now received as we drink from the waters of God's Spirit. As we swim, our once upright position of self-exaltation is changed for a horizontal posture of the

God My Banner

acceptance of God's will.

The mysteries of the deep and the enchantment of being submerged in the waters of the Spirit will make work seem like play. Then, we will look back upon our awkward life above water and question why we did not accept the invitation to swim sooner. We must leave our shores of past hurts and sorrows to embark upon the journey of the Spirit.

From this time on, I was without a mentor. My reputation was ruined. Congregation members were followed and yelled at in public places. I was not welcome in some very well known churches. My confidence was shaken. Things seemed beyond repair.

Most of the ministers that contributed to my troubles were the very ones that would stir the people for an hour on Sunday, preaching about the crisis in African America. While decrying the violence, they would with their tongue, cause more pain in this young black man than a shotgun ever could.

Many such events shook my faith. I was too young to have learned the lesson of David, **"I was young and now I am old, yet I have never seen**

Out of Africa

the righteous forsaken . . . "(Psalm 37:25) Our banner may be tattered and torn but the truth for which it flies will always triumph, if we cling to it in precious faith.

Truth cannot be bent, only broken but truth crushed to the ground will rise again.

SIX

GOD WHOM I WORSHIP

The biblical definition of worship is very different from the way the word is commonly used today. Worship is a derivative of the old English word, worthship.[1] If we take apart the syllables of the older word, it is easy to understand what it means - to attribute worth to an object or person. Hence, the way the Christian worships God is mainly through our willing obedience to the Spirit and Word of God. Jesus said, **"If you love me, you will obey what I command." (John 14:15)**

Out of Africa

Abraham whom the Bible calls the father of the faithful is a towering example of a worshiper. In Genesis 22:5, he told his men that he was going up the mountain to "worship," yet he knew that he was to sacrifice his son. Obviously, his view of worship was different from much of the modern world. Many people casually attend church once a week and call it worship.

All of Abraham's years of faith culminated in this act of worship. This act became the Old Testament's clearest portend of what God would do with His own Son at Calvary.

Throughout my early years with Christ, Abraham has been the example that the Holy Spirit used, most often, to provoke me to a life of faith. Likewise, as the life of Abraham had a steady progression of circumstances that would prepare him to offer Isaac, events were occurring in my life, like the notes of a musical score that could not be complete without a dramatic crescendo. I have shared how God had become my redeemer, ordainer, sanctifier, vindicator and banner. Yet, all this was designed such that I could become a true worshiper.

In our age, God would not ask anyone to sacrifice their child on an altar. Yet, God is still in

God Whom I Worship

the business of receiving worship and asked me to offer to Him something almost as precious - my manly pride. Today, when I lift my hands to worship God it has great meaning. It is a profound sign of my surrender to the loving kindness of the soon coming King.

DILIGENCE

After spending eight years of my adult life at Howard University, it was finally time for me to leave. It was there that I had experienced so many of life's first. I had been both loved and eventually hated on this so familiar campus.

On many afternoons, it was difficult for me to swallow as I passed the students, laughing and frolicking, as they went about completing their education. I was ashamed of my poverty and of the fact that I was not permitted to finish my studies. Every day of ministry at Howard had to be preceded by a far reaching decision to do the will of God versus my own.

Frequently, as I walked across the campus with my Bible in my hand, I would grieve deep down inside for the lost souls and sometimes even for myself. As quickly as my glory days had come, they were gone. If a person, who once knew me, looked my way, it was often followed by a puzzled expression, as if asking themselves, "What happened to him?" It was a spiritual joy to meet the needs of the many young Christians on the campus but it was an intense emotional challenge for me to let myself be considered a failure, when I knew I could compete in the work place.

I had prayed more for that University than I had for myself. I loved those kids with all my heart. With little fanfare, my assignment was complete. It was time for me to move on.

Perhaps some of my most difficult moments as a campus minister were watching the friends that I came into school with marry and excel in their fields. Sometimes I felt trapped in the will of God with some of my most personal needs unattended. There are times when the answers to our smaller needs are delayed so God can meet our greater needs.

FLOWER BOX

One day during this time, God gave me a vision to help me understand His heart. I was inside a flower box picking flowers. I had several flowers in my hand. With an earnest expression on my face, I asked the Lord if I could have one of the flowers. The Lord responded with a delighted,

God Whom I Worship

"Yes." However, just three feet from the flower box, I saw Jesus laying with His face down on the grass. He was sobbing. The following morning, God said to me in a tender tone, "Even when you are old, you will still be my little boy."

I began to search my heart for the reason why Jesus had wept. Then He said to me, "I do not want to lose you." Finally, I began to understand why Jesus wept. The time was nearing when He would have to share His child with a wife, my flower. I Corinthians 7:32-33 explains His tears.

> **"I would like you to be free from concern. An unmarried man is concerned about the Lord's affairs - how he can please the Lord. But a married man is concerned about the affairs of this world - how he can please his wife."**

I am sure that as He cried, He thought of the proud day the Holy Spirit gave birth to a new baby boy, named Derek. Perhaps, He thought of the many times He held His frail child to His breast to feed him the milk of His Word. Maybe, He laughed as He remembered all the wild excuses I came up with when I did something wrong. Possibly, He remembered the amazed expression

Out of Africa

on my face, the first time I allowed His Spirit to gush through me, as I spoke in tongues. Maybe, He remembered the many moments of my life when I would stare into His Word with wide eyes, believing without question that all my Abba Father said was true. He is my Friend and has created in me devotion that only He can inspire.

As I persisted to seek God about my wife, a girl who had all the appearances of what a good man should avoid kept coming to mind in my prayer time. She was a confessing but uncommitted Christian.

During this time, God would constantly tell me to marry her. This troubled me. Unbeknownst to me, she had been telling her friends that she wanted to marry me. Eventually, I asked her out on a date. She told me, "This is a dream come true." God had been setting us up.

In spite of the lovely things I could imagine by faith, I did not want to marry her. This started to really bother me. After years of chastity, it was difficult for me to understand why God would send me to a woman with other lovers.

Only days after our first date, she slept with another man to get back at me over a

God Whom I Worship

misunderstanding. Soon, she was sleeping with even other men. Welcome to the nineties! I did not know what to do. Soon we were not seeing each other anymore. Yet, for almost a year afterward, I would hear God say over and over, "Marry her."

To be rewarded with such a woman after years of devotion was unthinkable. It was an ordeal for my pride to contain itself and not entertain the rationale, "If God is going to reward me with such a woman, what is the point of living holy?" Somehow, it did not satisfy me to remember that He told me, "Let no school say it trained you, let no man say he made you rich and let no women say she is your reward."

We are socialized to think that love between a man and a woman is the height of life. As a teenager I always had girlfriends. It was in these relationships that I could dull the pangs of my yearning for divine love. It is only the love of God that can ultimately satisfy the human soul.

It was as if God had been starving me from the only thing that I had ever received a feeling of worth from. Obviously the absence of a woman in my early years of faith was to cause me to learn how to find my self worth in Him alone.

Out of Africa

This situation with the young lady upset everything I knew about God. Twice, I attempted to quit the ministry and go back to a life of sin. However, something deep inside me would not allow it. Sometimes healing hurts.

QUESTIONS

I could not understand why God permitted this. In my thinking, this was not just a girl but my wife, sleeping with other men. Even as a sinner, I would not put up with that. This put a strain on my relationship with God like nothing else. After all, I expected that the wife God would bring me, would be the center of my joy. I overlooked the first commandment, **"You shall have no other gods before me." (Exodus 20:3)**

Theologians have long debated whether Hosea's (a prophet whose name is the Hebrew equivalent of Jesus) marriage to a prostitute was due to his own indiscretion or whether he was directed by God. Those that argue the former overlook the cross. The death of Christ did not need to be so brutal, except for one purpose - to dramatize to the onlookers the depth of God's love. Certainly, God could have picked a far less painful death for His Son, but He needed to pierce our callused hearts with the most poignant proof of love possible.

God Whom I Worship

After over a year of standing in faith for her to have a closer walk with Jesus, I began to hear the words, "I am married to the backslider" (Jeremiah 3:14). In other words, God stays committed to those who forsake their commitment to Him. He wanted me to learn to do the same. For the first time in my life, I began to understand the sufferings of Jesus as He waits for His bride, the Church (Revelation 21:9). I had waited for her as God has waited for you and me. Oh, "**I want to know Christ and the power of His resurrection and the fellowship of sharing his sufferings . . .**" **(Philippians 3:10)**

As seriously as the pain of circumcision must have impacted ninety-nine year old Abraham, this experience settled in my mind, the measure of God's unconditional love for His people. Yet, I must make a very important point here. God will never force His will on human beings. Even though God may speak into our hearts His will for our lives, its fulfillment is not predetermined beyond our participation. Friendship, marriage and every virtue are things that are subject to our free will.

Throughout the year, I approached God with Mark 11:24, "**Therefore I say unto you, what things soever ye desire, when ye pray, believe** that ye receive them, and ye shall have them." (Mark 11:24 KJV) His response was always the same, "Son, you do not desire her." In other words, the condition for me receiving her from the hand of God was that I first desire her. By the grace of God, I was eventually released regarding this young lady. However, Jesus is always ready to receive anyone who would return to Him.

God knew the end of this situation from the beginning. He knew how both of us would respond. He never intended for us to be literally married but was challenging me spiritually to become more like Him. Abraham had a similar situation. Ultimately, he was not required to physically sacrifice Isaac but his willingness made it as good as done in God's eyes.

"¹⁰Then he reached out his hand and took the knife to slay his son.
¹¹But the angel of the Lord called out to him from heaven, 'Abraham! Abraham!' 'Here I am,' he replied.
¹²'Do not lay a hand on the boy,' he said. 'Do not do anything to him. Now I know that you fear God, because you have not withheld

God Whom I Worship

from me your son, your only son.
¹³Abraham looked up and there in the thicket he saw a ram caught by its horns. He went over and took the ram and sacrificed it as a burnt offering instead of his son." (Genesis 22:10-13)

I am sure that God's eyes were sharply focused on the events that would happen in Palestine that day. Abraham had heard the voice of God, ate with the angels of God, and even saw the similitude of Father and Son as a lamp and furnace (Genesis 12:1; 18:2; 15:17). Now Abraham was put into a situation were he had to believe in a God that raised the dead.

Abraham was promised that through the seed of Isaac, God's covenant would be established (Genesis 17:21). Isaac did not yet have children, so Abraham must have believed that the God who told him to slay his son, would also resurrect him (Hebrews 11:19). God had promised me that I would be married but after this episode in my life I began to give up hope.

I did not understand that resurrection can only happen after the flesh dies. Once He destroyed my boyish pride, He intended to resurrect my self-esteem and give it a greater glory. Worship is the only thing that can make boys into men.

SWEET SUCCESS

By the time I was finally released regarding the young woman I have been discussing, my church had moved out of Washington, D.C. The challenges mentioned in this book were too much for most of my D.C. congregation. The church had been meeting for about one year and was split right down the middle. Half of the church had sent a representative to give me a list of grievances.

They felt that the church had been growing too slowly. In the first year, we grew from six to just a little under thirty. Furthermore, some of the congregation began to follow strange notions about prosperity that were contrary to scripture - the fact that I was single, did not own my own home, that the church was still meeting in hotels without the money to build a church facility and that I had been alienated by some members of the church community was cause for me, as they put it, to "face the facts." They called me a failure and frankly, I could only agree with them. We canceled our contract with the hotel and I resigned.

God Whom I Worship

The next Sunday, a few people showed up at my apartment. They told me that they knew that God had called us to be a church and would show up every Sunday at my apartment, until I resumed my pastoral duties.

A few weeks later, two congregation member rented a house for me that was large enough for us to hold Sunday morning meetings. I moved from my apartment in Maryland to the suburbs of Virginia.

After about a year of meeting in my living room, I gained the courage to rent a hotel room in Virginia for Sunday service. We all felt that we were only in the permissive will of God to have meetings in Virginia but with all the bad memories in D.C., we did not want to go back. Things seemed hopeless.

Then, like the morning sun peeking over the horizon, the Lord finally said to me, "As with Job, I gave the devil the last five years of your life to do all that he could, save take your life. Now, I will reward you for maintaining your integrity." Perhaps God allowed me to confront and slay so many dragons from the outset, so that my future would not be dominated by a fear of them.

Out of Africa

A few days after this, my car stalled. It was about five years old and this was becoming a frequent occurrence. However on this occasion, the Lord told me to take the car to a dealership. I batted my eyes for a few moments but when the car restarted, I obeyed. After I parked the car at the dealership, it would not restart.

With nervous perspiration dripping from me, I test drove a sports car and filled out the credit application. I did not have a major credit card or regular income but by the grace of God, I was somehow approved. I left with a brand new car.

Just a few months later, the Lord told me to write an article. I wrote it and felt led to have it submitted to the Howard University student newspaper. It was printed and soon the editor began anticipating my submissions. I began to reach more students in my absence from the University than I did while I was present. By the end of the year, my articles had been published in three African American college newspapers, reaching over twenty thousand students.

As Job gained twice as much as he had before his trial, my faith had withstood the test of time and God began to bless me like no other period in my life (Job 42:10). Remember, the blessings of Job can only follow the perseverance of Job.

> "As you know, we consider blessed those who have persevered. You have heard of Job's perseverance and have seen what the Lord finally brought about. The Lord is full of compassion and mercy."(James 5:11)

ENTER A QUEEN

In May 1993, seven months after I was released regarding the first young lady, I drove two young ladies from my congregation to the beauty supply store. They noticed that the young woman behind the counter was smiling at me. I was embarrassed but I could not help but smile back. She was gorgeous.

Later, they returned to the store without me to find out if she was a Christian. When my birthday came around, the young ladies brought the pretty little sales clerk to my house for a barbecue that they were having for me that evening. The next week, we went out on our first date. I was interested but was being very cautious.

Out of Africa

This young lady was in the Virginia area to take care of some personal matters. She was planning to return to school in California in a few months but love did not follow her plans. A few months later, I proposed. At first, she told me no because she was planning to go back to her college on the West Coast.

We kept seeing each other and finally she decided to wear the engagement ring, but on her right hand. She told me that she loved me but she would not marry me until I had received her father's approval. I figured that if she still honored her father and he was on the other side of the world, she would also be an honorable woman for me.

A few weeks later, her father came to town and I asked him for her hand in marriage. He had been asked this before by other callers but to the shock of most of her family, he gave me his approval. Four months later, we were married.

God by His tender mercies had reached His arm all the way to Africa to fulfill His promise to me. God's eyes spanned the oceans, mountains, valleys and plains to bring me more than I could have ever acquired for myself. He brought this comparably banal New Yorker, an Ethiopian

God Whom I Worship

Queen. Only God has the power to bless so perfectly.

By the way, I am six years older than my wife. I married at twenty-eight. If God had answered my prayer at twenty-four, Yeromitou would have only been eighteen. We both needed more time to grow before we married. All the time I was wringing my hands over receiving my marriage partner, God was on the other side of the world preparing her.

Seven months after our marriage, we purchased our first home. As we watched the builders add each floor to our three story townhouse, we imagined God building our future. A few months after we moved into our home, my wife left her job and began to work with me in the ministry.

Then in a master stroke, God spoke to my heart and the members of our church that it was time for us to go back to Washington, D.C. and fulfill His plan for us there. Another seven months after my wife and I moved into our new home, we renovated our first store front church building in Washington D.C. Humble acorns become the greatest oaks.

Out of Africa

When I returned to the city, I was no longer the timid young man that had been chased away. I felt that I had faced the worst of circumstances and survived. I was afraid of no man and ready to defy any devil.

In the first two months of our return to D.C., our church more than doubled in size. We expect to outgrow this facility within our first year. However, as enjoyable as these things may be, their receipt is not the moral of my story. The fortune that ten years in Christ has gained this young African American cannot be purchased with money or by any other means. My treasure is best voiced by the words of David, **"I was young and now I am old** (older), **yet I have never seen the righteous forsaken or their children begging bread." (Psalms 37:25)**

CONCLUSION

It would be a grave error for me to conclude that faith in Jesus Christ erases the fact that I am an African American and my responsibilities to my community. It does something far greater. It elevates people of every race to a plane higher than racial distinctions - righteousness in Christ.

Amid our diversity, God creates unity through His people recognizing a single truth,

God Whom I Worship

"For all have sinned and fall short of the glory of God and are justified freely by his grace through the redemption that came by Christ Jesus." (Romans 3:23-24) More simply put, every age, all races and both sexes have proven themselves shamefully inadequate when compared to the excellence of His eternal glory. Yet through His love, He lifts all of humanity to be free from the power, guilt and penalty of sin.

I have not written this book in an ivory tower. I have needed God's grace as much as the next person. However through faith and patience, I have come to understand that Jesus loves me, even black me, as much as anyone else.

In the barrio, He has a marvelous Spanish accent. In the hood, He gestures with the grandness native to the culture. On the reservations, His Spirit soars like the eagle and He dances enthusiastically to the rhythm of the drum. Throughout North America and the world, Jesus is greater than our differences. He loves us so enormously that if only for a moment we could grasp the height, depth and width of it, our present bodies could no longer contain our spirits and souls. Until that day, if we would walk in just a measure of His love, we can change our world for Christ.

Out of Africa

When I began to work on this manuscript, the Holy Spirit said to me, "As I have called your bride *out of Africa*, so shall I call mine. **"The Spirit and the bride say, 'Come!' and let him who hears say, 'Come!' Whoever is thirsty, let him come; and whoever wishes, let him take the free gift of the water of life.'" (Revelation 22:17)**

Pray With Me

PRAY WITH ME

Heavenly Father, I believe that Jesus Christ is Your Son and died on calvary's cross for my sin. I believe that on the third day He arose from the dead with all power in His hand. I ask You to use that power to save me and make me more like Jesus.

If you have prayed this prayer and believe it with your heart, Romans 10:9 declares that you are saved: **"That if you confess with your mouth, 'Jesus is Lord' and believe in your heart that God raised him from the dead, you will be saved."**

I would like you to sign your name and write today's date and time in the space provided below so that you can always remember the day and the hour that your name was written in the Lamb's Book of Life.

Write us and let us know about the wonderful decision you have made and we will send you information that will help you begin your walk with Christ.

_____

Name   Date   Time

NOTES

Chapter 1 - God My Redeemer

1. Franklin, John Hope and Alfred A. Moss Jr. <u>From Slavery to Freedom</u>. New York: Alfred A. Knopf, 1988, 28.

2. Gibb H.A.R. and J.H. Kramers eds. <u>Shorter Encyclopedia of Islam</u> Ithaca, N.Y: Cornell University Press.

3. Vol. 1 Hadith no. 63

4. Vol. 9 Ibid no. 242

5. Vol. 1 Ibid no. 662

6. Vol. 9 Ibid no. 162

7. Sura 3:47; 4:157

8. Sura 5:75-77; 4:116

9. Sura 9:29

10. Sura 4:34

11. <u>Gibb H.A.R. and J.H. Kramers eds. Shorter Encyclopedia of Islam</u> Ithaca, N.Y: Cornell University Press.

12. Sura 4:3

13. Vol. 2 Hadith no. 541

14. Gunton, Berry W. <u>Foxe's Book of Martyrs.</u> Old Tappan: Fleming H. Rewell Company., 7 & 9.

Chapter V - God My Banner

1. Sura 62:5

Chapter VI - God Whom I Worship

1. <u>Webster's New Collegiate Dictionary</u>. Springfield: G & C Merriam Company, 1981, 1342.

HAM PUBLISHING COMPANY

Ham Publishing Company is the communications arm of Derek Grier Ministries. Through print and other forms of mass communication, Ham Publishing Company is committed to excellence as we win our world for Christ.

If you would like to be added to our mailing list or order another copy of *Out of Africa* write or call:

DEREK GRIER MINISTRIES
P.O. BOX 73308
WASHINGTON, DC 20056-3308
(800) 841-7963
(202) 265-9827

NOTES